Vacationland

poems by

Michael Lee Bross

Finishing Line Press
Georgetown, Kentucky

Vacationland

Copyright © 2023 by Michael Lee Bross
ISBN 979-8-88838-320-9 First Edition
All rights reserved under International and Pan-American Copyright Conventions. No part of this book may be reproduced in any manner whatsoever without written permission from the publisher, except in the case of brief quotations embodied in critical articles and reviews.

ACKNOWLEDGMENTS

The author would like to acknowledge with deepest thanks the publishers and editors of the following publications for their generous work, within which some of this book's poems previously appeared.

"Las Vegas, Nevada," "Summer Vacation," and "The Magic Kingdom," *CHAOS: Poetry Vortex,*
"Niagara Falls," *Trees in a Garden of Ashes*
"Centralia, Pennsylvania" *Northeastern Poetry Review*
"South of the Border" *Best Emerging Poets of Pennsylvania-2019, Z Publication*
"Vacation Slide #1" "Vacation Slide #2," *30th Anniversary Mobius Poetry Magazine*
"Six Flags, New Orleans," *Houseboat*

Publisher: Leah Huete de Maines
Editor: Christen Kincaid
Cover Art: Adrienne E. Bross—Alpine Mountain, 2020
Author Photo: Adrienne E. Bross
Cover Design: Elizabeth Maines McCleavy

Order online: www.finishinglinepress.com
also available on amazon.com

Author inquiries and mail orders:
Finishing Line Press
P. O. Box 1626
Georgetown, Kentucky 40324
U. S. A.

Table of Contents

Steeplechase Park, New York xi

I.

Vacation Slide #1 1
Niagara Falls, NY 2
The Magic Kingdom 4
Sandrock Wishing Well, Annapolis Maryland 5
Venice Beach, California 8
Heaven's Peak, Montana 9
Vacation Slide #4 11
Summer Vacation 12
Yellowstone National Park, Wyoming 13
Waikiki, Hawaii 14
Shea Stadium, Queens New York 15
South of the Border, South Carolina 17
Hadley Creek, Illinois 18
Vacation Slide #8 22

II.

Vacation Slide #2 25
Philadelphia Museum of Art, Philadelphia, PA 26
Homestead Crater Hot Springs, Midway Utah 28
The House on the Rock, Dodgeville Wisconsin 30
Interstate 81 South 32
Epcot Center 34
La Brea Tar Pits, Los Angeles California 35
Wonderland Running Trail, Mount Rainer Washington 36
Vacation Slide #3 38
Roswell, New Mexico 39
Minneapolis, Minnesota 40
Universal Studios, California 41
Salem, Massachusetts 43

Vietnam Memorial, Washington, DC 45
The Rock and Roll Hall of Fame, Cleveland, Ohio 46
The Holy Land Experience, Orlando Florida 47
Interstate 80 West 48
Atlantic City, New Jersey 50
Centralia, Pennsylvania 51
Interstate 76 East 53
Lewis Ginter Botanical Garden, Richmond, VA 55
Summer Vacation 56
Vacation Slide #5 57
Route 23, New Jersey 58

III.

Vacation Slide #6 63
Liberty Science Center, Jersey City, New Jersey 64
The Poconos, Pennsylvania 66
Las Vegas, Nevada 68
O'Hare International Airport, Chicago 69
Storyland, Glen, New Hampshire 71
Legotown, New York 72
Vacation Slide #7 73
Disney's Hollywood Studios 74
Summer Vacation 76
Six Flags, New Orleans 78
Seaside Heights, New Jersey 80
Interstate 95 North 81
The Animal Kingdom 83
Gettysburg, Pennsylvania 84

Epilogue
Cedar Point, Ohio 87

My Unending Thanks 89

About the Author 91

For Virginia Bross,
gentle, eternal strength

Steeplechase Park, New York

To inquiring Friends: There was a lot of trouble yesterday that I have not had to-day, and there is lots of troubles to-day that I did not have yesterday. On this site will be erected a bigger, better Steeplechase Park. Admission to the Burning Ruins—10 cents.
  ~George C. Tilyou, Owner Steeplechase Park, 1907

Come One, Come All!
Come Back, Come Back!
To Steeple Chase, the Funny Place!
Come flocks of tomorrow!
Come dream! Come Eden!
Come into the lights on the edges of the sea,
        and taste of the garden our apple seeds grew!

Thrill to the Airship Tower, tickle the fancy of Heaven!
Behold oddities and miscreants at the Human Zoo!
Rocket off along our 'Trip to the Moon' and the utopia city of the cosmos!
Dare the Human Roulette Wheel! Spin suicidal, cast off from the revolutions!

For this chase of paradise is a race run in circles,
a wonderland sheltered in the smile of a feral doll,
a 10 cent Brick Bat trick! You've been had, but you laugh
like Sylvester Meade, downing Royal Crown Cola and Hershey bars!

Come forever Summer! Come all, the internal and beautiful,
marvel at the sacred Concert Salons and Ballrooms!
Cry out in a romping Vaudeville burlesque, fling the chemises and corsets!
Gay and sin as you trip the light fantastic— straight into the fires at the end of the world!

For this night here, here, you are *L'Allegro*, here, you are angels!
And perhaps here we will burn holy, burn beautiful and alone as God always intended! Or perhaps here, this night, we will dine in-between the very cracks of Rapture!

I.

Vacation Slide #1

This picture from home
always somewhere tropical
sand under the sun

The clouds are eating the sky
as waves pace God's even breath

Call of gulls echo
Tiny Ark, tempest-littered branches
driftwood painted blue

No breeze. Beached boat at world's end
We are not in this photo

Niagara Falls, NY

Today is today, but like most days, I am not where I am.
I am on vacation. Michael Bross is the Billy Pilgrim of Pennsylvania.

Today, it's 1997, and we're driving through Ramapo, making for New York State. It's 11pm, and New Jersey is made of traffic and taillights. Paul loves how the road doesn't talk. My Rush mix on the radio, and Paul just drives. He talks about QVC Christmas presents. I talk in circular nonsense about time travel and how I can't play the real drums but am the best air-Neil Peart south of Toronto.

Today is 1991. My father is buying me my first bass guitar for 50 bucks. The pick-ups are shot, the action is an inch off the frets. Unplugged and without sound, I blister my fingers and grow out my ponytail to look like Geddy Lee.

Today is 2011. Paul's giving me his father's computer monitors that are full of cigarette smoke. Paul's father is dead; he doesn't talk about his dad. I don't either. He has no need for his father's junk anymore.

Today is 1994. Paul is shy, builds sound systems out of scratched car speakers in his basement. 26-point stereo sound for Star Wars movie nights and Mortal Kombat-Pong marathons. We meet weekly to play Dream Theater and Rush covers. His father builds amplifiers, and Paul plays the drums I can only fake. At 10 o'clock, we stop being loud and play Sega past midnight.

Today is 1995. Paul the senior leaves town with a stripper from *Winner's Go-Go*. His wife smokes on her couch and cries to the Television how love has made her grave. The QVC tells her to act now before the offer is gone forever.

Today is 2001. I sink the lead doll of my father into the ground. Paul drives me to work. Too early to talk, the light of the sun burns our eyes as he drives.

Today is 1945. Billy Pilgrim wants out of Dresden, so he leaves for outer space.

Today is 1997, and we're driving through Ramapo, making for New York State. It's 11pm, and Paul wants to drive to Niagara; I laugh and dare him. He shrugs, calls my bluff, and I fold just short of Palisades. Paul loves how the road never speaks, even as I keep us in the country of our forefathers, a country of waterfalls. Niagara: America's jumping-off point, where we all line up the river, thump the barrel and dive, desperate for destinations to our cascade, looking for a view of Canada, to know our fathers' country ends somewhere, even as it crashes into a river the shape of the entire sky in reverse. And for the length of our fall, we see that the threat to our borders is our borders—borders we love and fear both more than God.

Today is today, and so it goes. I write poems on Paul's father's monitor about vacations I never take.

And today is 1998. Paul is driving for Niagara, his passenger seat full of mix CDs and empty space. He'll make the border by dawn, just in time to see the sun rise out of the water.

The Magic Kingdom

The day Dad got AIDS
we're plucked from school and packed
into a Geo Prism, with the Goofy plushies,
and overnight bags, a pilgrimage into the sun,
counting the distance from home in license plates
and the scroll of the pink and caramel sky.

Body heat burns us to sleep,
heads rested in the hammocks of the seatbelt,
dreaming car windows are Monorail's Plexiglas,
Fantasyland rising in a halo of lost balloons,
a triage of mouse ears and the damaged souls of vacationers,
who come for the Miracles of this Wizard Walt,
idol in brass, miracle man on a pulpit of awe,
were we congregate in a mass
circling in wishes, a fanfare of the fatal,
wheelchairs whisked to the front,
first in a fiction of flight.

"Come children of the world to this happy place!
Come oh limping, oh amputated,
Oh lonely and polluted!
Dream of magic mountains, scented in chlorine,
and living cartoons. Dream of sing-song parades
Oh you hitchhiking ghosts!"

And come night,
with captured stars in sorcerer hats,
we'll have forgotten, sold absence in Spectromagics,
dancing brooms sweeping away the debris of our days.
Sweep clean the blood and lost limb
Sweep clean into picture frames
Where we are invulnerable,
asleep in the hammock
of my father's arms, starving
while dining on the food of dreams.

Sandrock Wishing Well, Annapolis Maryland

Each night,
I dream the baby
fell into the well,
fell into a black spot
with only a thin pin of light,
lodged in the throat of the world.
she can see me, cries a sound like "daddy,"
till she falls asleep and leaves the body
to the earth's wet belly.

~

As a boy, the wells
would run dry,
400 feet plus
the grip of stone,
toilets rasped,
the sinks spat air
dry and sick
on the emptiness of depth.
We would toss pebbles
down the neck,
Check the depth
counting Mississippi's
till the stones hit the bottom,
as if you could wish with rocks
or drink wishes, flipped coins
the duex ex machina
of desperate boys
who thirsty even now
remember we bury the dead
in the ground we drink from

~

Mother says she keeps death
Closer than any dream.
She keeps it to her skin
messes it in her hair— a dirty soap.

"I gave death to my children
The day I gave birth,
The way I hang baskets, empty
from the kitchen ceiling
with hooks because the only way
to carry love is to keep
space ready for it.
It's safer to know what is missing
than to know what is there."

~

It's simply a matter of facts:
January 26th, 2001
Pinkel Funeral Home
It's 3pm, and the temperature feints a rise above freezing.
The lead doll is dressed in a soft gray suit.
I slip a ring marked "Faith" into his pocket,
and my kiss hits cement.
The doll's mustache is still, head slick like a wet ball,
formaldehyde bones,
polyurethane skin
the color of turkey gizzards varnished for Television.
His rotting has stopped,
Boxed to be shipped like luggage to the grave,
and we mourn like scenery.
The facts are simple—
Dad is dead
And I don't go to the cemetery.
The grave, the ground, this earth
is of no importance.
Just sink the lead into the soil,
And let the well-water begin to drink

~

My sister and I have picnics
on the dirt driveway near the well.
We have sand and butterfly cocoons
in teacups, pretending to drink
dryness for real thirst.

We play Belladonna for blackcaps,
stained red, bringing berries to our lips,
as mother hangs wet curtains
from the clothesline,
slaving at stains and pressing
against the wrinkles made by the wind.

~

Adrienne, you never sleep well
when I am not in the bed.
Your mind makes record skips
in the dark; you think
I am an empty space—
only begging to be filled.
Death asks me every day
what time is good for me?
I reply anytime,
I will finish today, or never.
I was told death is somewhere
Between witness and faith.
Which is true
of everything else as well

~

Each night,
I dream the baby fell into the well,
Fell into a black spot with only a thin pin of light,
Lodged in the throat of the world.
she can see me, cries a sound like daddy,
till she falls asleep and leaves the body
to the earth's wet belly.

Venice Beach, California

Dad's dead weights
& a muscle beach VHS—
In the sandless sunless beach
of his basement, my father drips
coconut tanning oil in his sweat,
Weights clank
like a muted bell, ring
like a cut deadline.
His brace & thrust
a scream the sound
of a bench press.
His push hard enough to
redefine the body,
grunt enough to bleed
the heat out of blood,
build a healthy body
borrowed, not his own.
Maybe a flex proves strength
fit to fuck like teens too young
to hear their own hearts.
Maybe muscles give power
To punish the body,
pushing, tearing, wrenching
muscle that needs again and again
the pressure in the temple.
Push, push into the white-out
of pain, and maybe
Healthy is an act
He can survive.
Pushing restless
listening to a pulse
beating against the eardrum,
wondering when it will stop.

Heaven's Peak, Montana

Maybe I was looking
for something to see the future,
Maybe I sensed a warning
blurred out in the distance,
needing clarity.
Maybe I needed binoculars
To look as far away as I could.
I can't remember—
and it's hard to tell at thirteen.
So maybe I was just looking for porn,
rummaging through my father's closet.
He's off hunting, dreaming to kill
on peaceful Montana mountain tops,
just another survivalist who hates the taste of blood.
Seeking to witness heaven and the earth
in one mangled view—

So I take a scavenger hunt of what
I shouldn't find:
tanning oil (Coconut blend),
Steppenwolf cassette (tape snapped)
free weights (55 lbs)
hunting clothes that smell like pot—

I want to stop,
this instance, this shift
Stop the contamination,
Break the infection sight.
The incubation started here—

—insurance cards, (20 % co-pay)
lab reports, (K< 2.6 mEq/L)
T-Cells counts and opportunistic pathogens
"Living With HIV" pamphlets—

So I close my father's closet,
and learned not to learn.

No binoculars. No porn.
If you deny long enough
you'll make everyone immortal,
despite just one peak
at heaven hunting
from under the skin,
in the veins,

laughing.

Vacation Slide #4

Tried to catch water
in a photo, and it blurred
Kids in fountain blurred

Children of umbra at play
Picture too dark for faces

Rain caught falling up
distorts the start of the ground
with a leaky hand

Slippery motion distorts,
only honest state of light

Summer Vacation

And you will shine, like gold in the air of summer
    ~Kings of Convenience

It was an act of artistic vandalism
that sunk the jungle gym to the lakebed.
Her and I would paint ghost children in the ripples,
Translucent and optical dances among the trout and tadpoles
I'm an awkward wretch trying to stand tall in my teenage thinness
watching her in a teenage swimsuit, curves new to us both,
slender slide of her waists into their hips,
belly pink and freckled from the sun
the forest full of warning signs of bears and deer ticks
and sharp rocks below the cliff drops.
Sawmill Lake and a submerged jungle gym, broke in through
the steel yellow gate, parked on the side of Route 23.
The beach closed; the monument closed, we take the deer trails,
Skin scratched by the briar net of bare cedar branches—
This first summer, we learned to swim together,
This lake is a kind of sex, a movement of filling
and fluid currents. Swimming, we pool together
in the share of water between us—Yet I mistake her for a hunter's gun—
sleek and lethal, cheeks cooled, she becomes both crush and kiss,
both black caps and bittersweets in early summer heat.
Even then, I think there's AIDS in the water, and I beg the lake
to let me walk the surface, beg for dead wood to survive,
Even then, I saw bodies in the bog—
the jungle gym just a reflection chased underwater.
Even then, I'd have loved to drown
in pretend, forget the ripples and the frame of Sawmill.
My grip slips off her waist, and I swim away laughing,
Wondering how warm she must be in sun.
This is why we vacation here; the act of our embrace
might just save us both if we beg from rivers and ponds.
And maybe know rest and electricity as one
single moment.

Yellowstone National Park, Wyoming

Mom rocks in a chair as she paints from a paused VHS, no sound but the wood
in the walls. She tells me not to sleep on the couch; I'll ruin the presentation.
She paints Glacier Rock, perched, as if to roll, to track the glacier
That caved and abandoned it for the atmosphere. A boulder balanced, crushed
waiting for tourists. Her hand drinks the paint, pulls the color from the TV,
skin sucks out the pigment like fruit too long on the vine.

Our family carved our names in the block boulder the excavators left
exposed in the backyard, a loose tooth in the house foundation
back when the mortar was still wet, the framing boards still tree bones
waiting for the saw. There's blood in that wood, and when dad went cold,
his name was still in the rock; his path carved us a ravine
winds and rapid waters left us staring
at tourism videos and sweeping shots on the Travel channel.

Mom look. These vacations we never took—Inspiration Point, Artist's Point—
the Earth is an embrace, a river wiser than God and a smell like sulfur.
Steam is pain, sweet fuel to the geysers that cry as the planet knows we should.
Stone knows we crack and fissure under pressure and that it is not only the path
of glaciers carving landscapes that threaten our foundation—
but it's the foundation itself that will swallow us.

Mother, I love you and know why you paint pictures of rocks. I too want the
ground we once remembered to mimic a sense of standing once stable,
to catch and hold still the spin of the Earth so the rock won't tip.
Vacations are better not taken, preserved in paint and waiting.
But in your painting, I am a bird, an osprey, gray against gray,
cracking beak on stone in a faint rain of pebbles and sand—
paralyzed in paint by the changes in the wind.

Waikiki, Hawaii

My grandmother hums Jim Nabor's "Christmas in Hawaii,"
the one with Carol Burnett and Tom Selleck, where no one works or gets sick
save for Bobby Brady with his styrofoam idol curse.
Grandma gift wraps while keeping up on dishes and kitchen garbage.
Pruned, her hands sting at the nail beds.

Mark this Christmas of '92, before Santa stopped the con,
before I swallowed my want for Snake Eyes like a summer break-up.
We videotaped the dog to keep the camera off dad as he died
in the corner by the stockings wearing a Hawaiian Shirt and coconut tanning
oil in December, the gifts unopened, wrapping grief we never give out loud.

See, Hawaii 's an imaginary color we use to make beautiful New Jersey.
Where we have no sun, only a heat lamp, and highways strangle like warring
snakes through Rt 23's dirty Franklin Kar-Parts and abandoned Wayne movie-
marts, through After Dark strip clubs blacked out in the off-street shame of
Newark down Rt 9's dives, into Elizabeth and the ports of lost Chinese shipping
crates, into the port of our smog-water landfills full of wrapping paper.

But we are afraid of Hawaii and never travel to Waikiki, avoid its empty gas
stations and human pavement, blind ourselves to our shared human rust,
because white families need luaus and peaceful dream, the taste of the gods'
food, the roll of waves on warm sand to surf. We fear the need to remember our
currents, to remember our need for fire in our dance and discard Hawaii for
the flowers at the gate after the long, long flight, fleeing the flooding night into
the chase of the sun.

The Waikik iwe want is Jim Neighbor, on TV, at Christmas time in 1992,
where dad changes the channel to news of months old LA race riots,
and my grandmother asks, "Why can't they leave n------ along, their people
too!" We cringe and correct her with a hundred more polite variations
before we demand he turn the channel back.

Shea Stadium, Queens New York

Game 6 was the real game to watch.
Ojeda slipping in the first. Henderson's Homer,
Stanley's wild pitch and Mookie's Buckner grounder—
Game 6 was for a million replays packaged more neatly than the real.
If one picture is worth a thousand words, I slept through a million.

But he woke me for Game 7.
The score a safe 8 to 5, the chance for any dance of drama,
of any joint conquering of adversity safely surrendered—
a safe win in the bag and the last time we could play it safe together.
The living room dark but the cathorayed quiet light.
The timer already descending. Our world is a cave, but I clutched
his hand to my chest, stepped sleepy footed in pajamas.

One Out.
Romero pops a foul ball to Hernandez.
I squeal at the play, sleep gone.
He laughs at or with me, hands me my
little league glove as if I could shag
a fly ball from the living room.

Two Outs.
Boggs grounds weakly to Backman.
He didn't know yet, about the virus,
The receding blood, young and heroic, to me,
At 9 years old, his one leg makes him a pirate.
He watched me more than the game.

Three Outs
Marty Barret fans on a slider.
They dog-pile Orosco
We smile in the dark.
Even though I can't see him,
this one, this night, was good.

"This Crowd is ready to reach the Heavens!"

We cheer, wake up my sister who cried from a different dark room,
and he whispers us both quiet; I began to fall asleep,
this time for good, as he carried me back to bed…

and our ballgame
is over.

South of the Border, South Carolina

Let's pretend I'm nine.
The car bound for Florida, and I want to stop
because I like fireworks and alligator t-shirts,
because I like tacos, and my mother ate nine once
when she was pregnant with a me without limbs.

Let's pretend we drove through Pedro's crotch,
a 97-foot tribute to an American's Mexico.
A trap is baited for tourists with tamales,
friendly "banditos" the color of corn chips
smelling like gas stations
my dad says "beaner," and I laugh at beans
and it's okay because he had a Mexican friend once—

Let's pretend my dad is Cortez,
Roving the "Reptile Lagoon,"
instigating the snakes behind glass
that kill each other and suck down the conquered—
Dad drinking deep his racial supremacy
over snake-shit and the victor
who's choking to death on its brother's blood.

Let's pretend we're atop the "Sombrero Tower",
a pair of jerks on a burrow,
worried the cheap astray and toy Chihuahua
are as fake as they feel, wondering if
plastic knows we humiliate it with our ideas,
pose it ridiculous cartoons,
let our children chew on a mangled Mexico,

Just so we can pretend our vacations
are not behind the same side of the glass
as the rest of the reptiles.

Hadley Creek, Illinois

1.
Hunter's Code

When you kill a buck,
cradle the wound,
kiss his marble eyes
so he might glint a hint of love
as he goes.

Keep secret your name,
take the nickname Buck,
eat what you kill,
eat the muscle and horn,
become an organ made to hunt.
Keep secret your AIDS,
fuck strange women,
so they might carry your love
as she goes.

And if you bleed,
paint your son in stripes of war,
so he will remember
your face as the color red,
the color of love and raw meat
seen only in the bleeding.

2.
The Dream and the Earth

Run Buck run! Blood made of spiders!
Run Buck run! Bones demand a price!

Feet devolve to flippers.
Lungs to worms—
 back to gills.
liver to broth,
cells to sludge,

unable to be but prey,
less than animal,
less than meat.

The earth is full of faces
and teeth and lips like straws
drinks you—
primordial juice
spilling through gaps.

I've forgotten what it means to be prey,
to be food!
To meet teeth, faceless and without limbs!
To be in something's mouth!
To cry and be given no answer!

If we are to eat one another,
It is best to be meat in the stomach of spiders!

3.
Deer Rut

His dick is dry,
hung like a junkie
in mourning—
spent, ejaculated,
living in recovery.

He finds himself old,
depraved, flaccid at heart,
a limp flap of valves
rotting on fetish fantasies
and daydreams of his wife.

He answers to what
she won't touch
in groans, alone, naked but
a dirty shirt. From her
daughter's room, she says

"If sex could kill, it would."

His skin,
is a sack and wrinkle.
And he'll paint this room.
the color of the placenta,
into the warmth
He would penetrate
to remember.

4.

Scavengers and Gatherers

During warmer days
we would bathe
in Clove Brook
with bar soap,
just out of sight
of the overpass.

The house wells go dry.
The pool water
dirty with algae
& only good
for bucket water
used to flush
the toilet.

Upstream, Dad floated,
brook's puddled water,
leg stump bobbing
thick as bait
on a throne
of knee-high waterfalls.
Around him,
we'd gather wild fruit,
bruised on the stem,
in styrofoam beer cups

found along the creek banks.

Groveling in mud,
we'd drink from his stump—
blood belly-upped the trout
and made a thick soup
that we drank with both hands.

5.
Trophies

To strip the carcass,
   string up the hind legs,
display and dangle
   like a birthday piñata.
Gut the underbelly
   lengthwise with a single
cut, grip the intestines
   barehanded and forcibly
yank to spill the internal
   organs into the slop þucket.

Discard.

The blood will spill
   out in a flood, then
drip for hours.
   Knife the flank
into strip steaks
   & set to table.
Eat, with weak hands
   & desperate for salt.
Finally, mount the head.
   Take care to kiss
the eyes, that stare
   even past nightfall
no matter how much you beg
   for forgiveness.

Vacation Slide #8

In autumn, frail leaves
flutter to the lake surface,
plucked from their branches

A gate of rivers, calm wind,
no motion rushed or relaxed,

silent shared current.
still mirror, now holding breath—
microscopic waves.

Come winter, we seek stillness—
Or is it to freeze into place.

II.

Vacation Slide #2

Dad, the train is gone.
The rails shot straight for Eden.
Tracks, our steps in planks.

No rest. No stop. Just the ride.
Dustbowl flanks in black and white.

Blackbirds on the clouds,
a flock of pencil scratches
mark our migration.

The radio towers buzz.
Home some distance off the tracks.

Philadelphia Museum of Art, Philadelphia, PA

"Memory is more indelible than ink."
     ~Anita Loos

The portrait fades from color,
her face is firm
held tight for the wait of the flash
trying to look past the image.
          ~
Her face is firm,
held tight for the wait of the flash,
trying to look past the image
as if the future could look back
          ~
Held tight for the wait of the flash,
trying to look past the image
as if the future could look back
the flecks of paint off her face.
          ~
Trying to look past the image,
as if the future could look back.
The flecks of paint off her face
show the tan of cabinet card
          ~
As if the future could look back.
The flecks of paint off her face
show the tan of cabinet card
swallowing her out of thought and frame
          ~
The flecks of paint off her face
show the tan of cabinet card
swallowing her out of thought and frame.
The film, once primordial.
          ~
Show the tan of cabinet card
swallowing her out of thought and frame.
The film, once primordial
the way it holds time.

~
Swallowing her out of thought and frame.
The film, once primordial,
the way it holds time
as a suspension in liquid

~
The film, once primordial,
The way it holds time
as a suspension in liquid
till we are nothing but the color
of all things behind our eyes.

Homestead Crater Hot Springs, Midway Utah

The bath water

spills to the floor

as I submerge,

all sound dampened

in the clouded water.

I can't help

but sink,

skin dirt wash adrift,

alone in the hum

of heart currents,

pulse visible

in the ribcage—

touch of silence,

the whole of all things.

I think of water,

clean hot springs,

think of depth and try to float

in the blood

that floods the tub

to the floor,

from the gore

of our broken

well.

The House on the Rock, Dodgeville Wisconsin

Derealization disorder involves a persistent or recurring feeling of being detached from the surroundings (people, objects, or everything), which seem unreal. People may feel as if they are in a dream or a fog or as if a glass wall or veil separates them from their surroundings. The world seems lifeless, colorless, or artificial.
~David Spiegel, MD, Stanford University School of Medicine

The point from the beginning   was to become lost
at home   in a mind   in a house   on the rock—
with its chimera carousel   and   its robot music
with its tin tea set
and fabric family   snowmen
firearm forks spoons and   knives
a dinosaur   of stuffing a dollhouse under glass
with ventriloquist   dummies chewing   on air
and panic that I have forgotten what awake means

that the clocks are wrong melted
logic dim
                    ens
                            ion   al
      dream scape
that I am   an architect abandoning math
that   my mind's a projector rolling
a dancing doll jigging   stringless   shutters like a flip book
a two-dimensional   cartoon being   undrawn   into simple lines
until   it all   vanishes   along with the rotting
knick-knacks   a mismatch of a horder's   wrath   intimate
  plastic and glass menageries
                    that loves   like a telescope   loves   a   distant   moon

        for   years
i will wake up dreaming   here
     upon the rock
because father died   and took all
the *(help)* symbolism
                            with him,
because consequence is a nail

30

                        in the foot
                                    of   a   *(please help)*   god

as thin as sleep unwaking
who built   a house   on the rock
        that looks like a dream (no stop, please *stop*)
made of meaning
                    I no longer can touch

                a vacant   universe where
love is made

                            of   empty

                            unrelenting space

Interstate 81 South

5am is the time everyone dies
My grandfather, grandmother, father
All dying before morning.

Is that why we left for vacations
before dawn, at 5am, before the sun
shows us west with any certainty?

This was always our departing hour
Sleep glazed, animated bodies
Dreaming of sunshine and rest,

dreaming of the ocean
and land's end beyond this state
of emergency colored in traffic lights

along the Turnpike. Airplanes look to land,
descending seemingly onto the highway
and traffic of Elizabeth,

landing lights a singular flick of static
on a great gray screen,
owl eyes hunting the barrens

of dead cranes and cargo towers.
New Jersey, as if it could hold its breath
and know what radios say

without electricity to translate,
falls silent as we would drive south—
dead phone calls left on hold.

As we drive, I become invisible in pieces.
first the hand, then the chest
and head, clothes floating

on their own, down the exit ramps,
down the grass and concrete patches—
so slow, disintegrating from sight.

Because 5am is a time for dying
Which is what we do
on vacation, die for a time

hoping for paradise or perdition
hoping to sleep long enough
to miss the phone calls

as the last strays of traffic
runs out of gas, this afterlife of cars,
where those we left behind
are simply the sky, pulling farther
& farther away

Epcot Center

"Son, let me teach you about AIDS"
he says as he strips off his prosthetic leg,
stumbling into flora
shaped to Mickey Mouse.
Drunk on German beer,
he bleeds his lesson out his leg stump,
squirms in a bush, presses his face into needles,
so afraid of the cradle
made of vacations and cartoons
and a world showcased
in miniature, bordered by traffic
and ticket booths.
He is bleeding,
onto the flower beds and troll robots,
onto Mark Twain and our forefathers,
into *World Showcase Lagoon*
fireworks rain his saturation,
his semen, made sick and sexless, just
Illuminations and snapshot souvenirs,
sanguine Innovation fountains
swallow *Innovations* & imaginations
turned bloody by his *Body Wars*,
bleeding into the *Land*, the soil,
and the *Living Seas*
until security comes
dressed as tourists, smiling
as they drag him from the scenery
back to the hotel bed
covered in hidden Mickeys
we dream of from home,
while drunk, you piss yourself to sleep.
My father's lesson, the pigment of blood,
is a paint stained over all colors,
monochrome red shading parade drums,
blind in all eyes
but mine.

La Brea Tar Pits, Los Angeles California

Each night, mother
I dream of devolution,
Cro-Magnon, Gravettian cave dreams
Gibbon, bipedal hair, claws, and sinew.
till I die an ameba— life sludge and the tar of memory.

In my dreams, mother,
the clocks are all wrong, set to the wrong Age.
Crawling backwards, I check the time,
Out-age the viscous liquid of skin and bones
AIDS rots my father into.

Mother, you tell me I have his posture, his slouch,
how alike are the exhibits of our skeletons,
& it's hard to believe myself
in a world awake, decomposed to bone,
looking for meat in the monsters of evolution's past.

You tell me I'm father's genetic expectations,
His naked blood in the bathtub decaying,
Dementia eats his brain back to primordial slime,
Wondering when he'll be back to work and responsible,
tar in his eyes chewing, swallows, till all light fails.

Am I responsible mother?
or do I remind you of prehistoric street trash
& mashed asphalt? What we hope to discard
makes black silt, confused peat,
a mass of sloth, magpie, and sabre-toothed maws.

But don't be scared mother,
When I wake up, I'll shut up,
take vacations in the Tar Pits
& try not to slouch
   so you can take pictures
of me, with the dinosaurs,
   sinking, sunk—and happy
to buy the t-shirt as a souvenir.

Wonderland Running Trail, Mount Rainer Washington

My father was a one-legged carpenter
who could hoist board stacks
with two good arms and hop
with a prefect imbalance
up scaffolding, fake leg leaning
over the edge against
the weight of the load.
He was a man of shaking equilibrium,
who hated the sun he worshiped,
clinging to life with one arm
while shading himself from it with the other.
He always dangled between
the living and the dead,
stood on the planks for years
before he feed his leg up the thigh
to a Ryder Rending meat grinder.

No, he knew the tipping point
young, running on two good legs
beautiful through the garbage fields
and the tall grass, past the end
of the dirt roads
on the edge of town.
By god he could fly free,
a ten-year old cherub
who sunk his own father,
eaten by cancer and the war,
into the well of his own thirst,
a boy with life
out of order, who never saw
there is love before there is cruelness,
that there is heat and light
even before the death of stars,
that we all drink of the well
before we are drunk by the dark,
wet, ground.

He could run faster than any kid alive,
because there was shadow behind him,
chasing, color of nothing, always behind him,
nailed to every leg, to every love he carried
in two good arms left shaking hands in the dark—
but the hand shaking is a missing leg.
and we remember death, so loud
we forget the sound of how he lived,
how he ran in sunlight.

And I wonder
if he thought, in that moment,
to plunge his leg into the grinder
so his shadow let go,
to cast darkness into the metal
fangs of the monster,
to hobble away
mangled, laughing
with the blood of victory in his teeth,
free to carry and build
strong wood in August sunlight
sweating on the frames
of someone elses' home.

Vacation Slide #3

We make our own sky
cotton white atmosphere arch
planes in the windows

International gateway
minute mechanical flights

Glass Crystal Palace
no color but white and steel
to stain soft fake clouds

Yet so close to outer space
we're here, imitating birds

Roswell, New Mexico

Let's tell a truth here.

The day we are discovered by aliens
    will be an odd number, in the middle a partly cloudy
Tuesday, most likely in a bland month
    like March or September,

So we might miss the landing, even geeks like me
    feasting on Fat Boy Specials at Big D's
Downtown Dive, tipping back Cokes in tribute
    to alien life and the size of outer space,

cosplaying Coneheads, meeting Mulder
    and green skinned women in cosmic
carnivals and paranormal parades of inflatable
    Martians making for the gravity-free void.

Even we might miss the landing. For what weight this world
    insists upon us, what is left but to wish
to become alien, to know the nature of nothing
    and become pregnant moons in lonelier orbits?

So we rush 51, despite the threat,
    being machined down by the lead
at the gate, metallic shreds flesh back to Earth,
    dreaming scientific dreams, praying for anything alien,

But this weather balloon's crashed, alone in a darker sort of space
    our autopsy in the sand and without witness.
We wish space to be forever more than here,
    to make litter in the absence between stars.

So we might miss the landing, because the truth is this:
    There's a holy potential in UFO souvenirs,
because by god, hook or crook,
    I'm getting off this so-called island Earth.

Minneapolis, Minnesota

I grew up in a box, a glowing box of pirated VHS cassettes, a box adrift in space, a satellite of St. Paul public access comedy shows, cheezy sci-fi monstrosities and spandex space heroes. See I thought Minnesota was a postcard vacation, a vacation better when *not* taken, photos of scenery best captured in artistic angles than viewed from the highway. Because Minnesota is a vacation best taken within the sanctity of plot holes and weak character development, in budget movie space crafts. I'm 13 and have had enough of continuity. I want to live on the Satellite of Love. I want to be hugged, the way space hugs a satellite. I want my head to fall off, the way Tom Servo goes to pieces mid-scene and keep talking, a harmless broken gum ball machine. I want life to be full of cheap sets, *Space Mutiny* Lieutenant Lemounts who mans her post two scenes after eating lazer blasted death. Maybe I want to hear a director's voice spill into the foley, like in *Egah* warning me to "Watch out For Snakes!" so I can see behind the lens' eye, know there is at least some hack-job director at the helm of the whole ensuing train wreck. Or maybe it's knowing all the world's monsters are a made of cotton and flea market knick-knacks, a *Robot Monster,* a gorilla in a fishbowl with stiff joints and a face that never blinks. Minnesota is a vacation in frames of bad movies, where I'm with you, in love, in bed and tunneling though outer space and the atmosphere of someone else's breath without any moments at all. But I'm 13, and permeance and breath are no vacation. I'll never go to a Minnesota made of an Earth whose physics are consequence no postcard or box or satellite can ever escape.

Universal Studios, California

Simple and slow,
the boy takes kicks and fists to his fat body
in a bathroom stall, shoes stolen and flushed,
his classmates hold his head by his red hair,
smack his bent teeth against the urinal.

He cries, and between sobs
calls out for Spiderman to save him,
finding faith in comic books, still, at 17.
There is the expected rage, a natural selection

to bloody teenagers on my knuckles,
make them swallow teeth down their choked throats,
make Spiderman the violent reality
he certainly would need to be.

This is not about righteousness,
but religious in its need to beat against the cosmos,
beat at any eternal and wise entity who taught us to fear dark men
& darker fathers, calling us to fight in small corner stalls,

calling us to fight until we scream like babies
who believe in kindness, bought the rap
that the world welcomed us, threw us birthday parties
and cheered as we stumbled and outstepped our balance.

This is how we know cruelty is a natural act,
offending natural hands that pulp
another kid's vulnerable love of heroes,
who doesn't cry out for mother or god
but for cartoons and films franchises,
plastic collectables and Marvel movie t-shirts,

as classmates damage simple and broken brains,
like Spiderman fights crime by breaking bones,
how schools feed fat kids delicious beatings
from gangs of kids gleefully natural,
pummeling one another.

I want to break them and make myself cruel,
for god made every charity an evil,
my divine hand seeking to beat the cosmos
until it cries, until it knows a bullied boy
who believes in Spiderman—
just like me.

Salem, Massachusetts

In gray October,
I'm thin sleep and a skipped lunch,
walking a blistered foot in a tight work shoe
past the pageantry of inquisitions,
past the House of Seven Gables & Hauswitch Healing,
past kids in witch's costumes, laughing
marking the soil in hexes with a stick.

I said it once out loud, dad,
that I wish you were dead,
a flammable witch, a sin
I could celebrate, set ablaze & frolic free
among jack-o-lantern & autumn leaves
the color of blush and torches.
We make death macabre delights,
forget witches were women,
hysterical and sick on the mold
of old Bibles and older men.

But when I hear myself,
I sound so much like you, don't I?
My heavy air the phlegm in your lungs,
My stumble the stump of your walk.

When I wish you dead,
bedridden, wasted, empty of all but a pulse,
I see Salem gray is a pressed stone,
A confession piled till the chest crushes
but never caves from stones we carry—
home and hearth just wood and rocks
used for killing at our convenience.
To remove the burden darker thoughts,
To purge the sins in you
I see in me. Maybe,
if its okay with you dad, I'll play
outside your window for awhile,

as long as my Halloween doesn't drown
your dying out, your bleeding the color of the leaves.

Here, all the trees are the progeny of flame
Their guilt made of wood watching the fires burn.

Vietnam Memorial, Washington, DC

In the black glass,
your name is not there—
In the reflection
you are not there—

Instead you, who stole
a purple heart,
claimed your lost leg
shot off in Khe Sanh,
played a One-Winged
Pegasus and cheated a discount
from the flea-market army
store vendor with a bullet
shell in his eye.

Was it better to belly crawl
through Huong Hao
than to rip meat
in the Ryder Rending
of Matamoras, PA,
tripping into the grinder,
feeding it your leg
to chew from foot to thigh?

Was it better to bayonet Charlie
than to bed in a Port Jervis ER,
take AIDS through a Red Cross
donation? Was it better to burn
in Camp Carol than to fade away in a limp,
mundane intravenous drip?

This is why I can't look
in the black glass,
where your name— Lee Bross.
half a name I inherit
from you—
is not there.

The Rock and Roll Hall of Fame, Cleveland, Ohio

I have a guitar,
an empty chamber
crying sorrow, strings a labor
of knotted wood.
Mom gave it to me,
But did you know
you give away a hole,
a carved hollow hull,
chords choking the neck
in a fist, sound reverberates
down the roots to the tooth,
smacks like bare hands on a bat.
Break and throttle this neck,
I let strings dangle fretlesss—
skin strands on a nearly
severed limb.

This is the history of our music,
the music a mother gives a son,
manhood made of strings,
sex is a stage
we pray too,
die on
all for fame and silence—
Vibrate instead of feel,
Shake instead of sing,
because you can't speak
with a mouth full
of vibration,
you just vibrate
a violence we all mistake
for music.

The Holy Land Experience, Orlando Florida

Here,
Jesus is a musical,
a song and rhythm
breaking out around you.
He's a hand-shake at the Damascus Gates
He's a pair of t-shirts and shorts marked "Saved".
Here, Jesus is the Vegas River,
a baptism of clean chlorine, UV rated,
incense scented,
salt-white like me.
Jesus is washed breathable bright cotton,
a Kodak color cast-plaster Arc,
He's the Smile of the Child,
Jonah in a Styrofoam belly.
Here, Jesus is a 6-days-a-week crucifix,
a schedule pamphlet of prophetic events,
a Gethsemane Garden ShowTime.
Here, Jesus is a Wycliffe robot
translating the bible into the future,
into a Holy manufactured
portable litany of the electronic.
Why take back the Holy lands,
Full of blood and oil fire,
and skin colored warm and rich as dawn,
and nothing like us—

See Jesus,
I am dying of a deep well
and no taste to the water.
Faith is a fake sugar.
With our parents, or grandparents
we will turn the swamp to bog,
cloud the waters with bodies and claim
there's no bottom.
Because Jesus, I must see you bleed,
even if in corn starch over the Orlando concrete.
So we can experience Jesus yesterday—
today, and forever.

Interstate 80 West

What Nebraska knows of God
they know from the size of their sky

the torpid glare of the clouds
and its deep blue consuming

We are an irritant thread on the skin of God
riding the cut 80 slashes out through Omaha

abandoning Pennsylvania for Colorado
in a one-eyed Tercel

flea market freedom heaped
in the trunk & back seat

making for college in Fort Collins, life-absent of New Jersey,
making for our newlywed concrete apartment

with nothing more than the wedding presents in the gas tank
& a front seat full of motion sickness

our country is full of dirty and beautiful men
who would trade grace

for the absence of tracks
vanishing into the Nebraska grass

born driving from fathers who shout at the ground
& expect it to let go

who hope to be evaporate into borderless clouds
& rained back to the earth

We take pictures of the trip from behind the windshield
to make colorless mile-markers, fleeing west

but instead these are just our last known photos, dark Polaroids
in hues memories make in our head

memories mocking manhunts
hazes of bullets shot in a grainy film loop

50 miles from the Starkweather killing spree
who trailed dead family behind them

and driving west we try naming our love
in the snuff film we shoot of ourselves

in the Wyoming Badlands, dry eyes cry for forgiveness,
cry to live, but we still pull the trigger and smile

wondering where peace hides in the black
senseless night of Nebraska roads

that trail into nothing we know
like the World's last known photograph
as it tips off the edges of the map

Atlantic City, New Jersey

"Everything dies, baby that's a fact/ Maybe everything that dies, someday comes back/Put your make-up on, fix your Hair up pretty/ And meet me tonight in Atlantic City."
~Bruce Springsteen, *Atlantic City*

My grandmother would go to Atlantic City in September
to watch the shore and rescue the oceans swallowed keepsakes.
Her brittle steps in the sand sink and erase,
her hands held out to an empty space, looking for the end of her long walk.
But she's always been just another wood plank,
with a handbag full of Christmas angels and a forgotten fifty
squandered on the slots. Her son buried, and at 46, he never gambled.

She'd scratched her fingers for blood, 40 years on other people's clothes,
stitching thread under the dead desk lamps of Morley's Shirt Company
till she retired on social security and a $45 a month pension.
To live in our basement, stored with her boy like Christmas decorations.

That's why, she says, why it's about the wheel,
how the chrome marble dangles mercy
held in the spin. And that the spin is worth the loss
just for a breath's worth of chaos— hope, despite
the mathematical certainty of love nailed shut
in the graves behind her.

This time, let me win, just fucking once, let me win.
Let the firework burst be mine, the Independence Day of my reckoning,
let me know what it is to live as pure electric light.
But Atlantic City is built on a cliffhanger, on a flip, a bounce,
The World's Playground our family's chances
built on New Jersey sand, moist as a tongue this time of year.

She says *this world is prettier than I can handle.*
But, it's uglier too, and the Steel Pier eats neon and is always and forever
brighter than both of us. We're the Diving Horses betting on deeper water
or Taj Majal ghosts jumping with no lover but the approaching earth.

Centralia, Pennsylvania

Ashland is going to die next.
They say Centralia's coal fires
are burning out its organs,
beneath the complexion of her carbon skin,
beneath the dirt, beneath the cracked pavement
we are burning in a silent vein of hell
the earth hugs, like a mother in heat
this earth we've carved into veins
so we could vanish like smoke, now
less than the light we recall of the surface,
less the sight of Sylvania headlights
spotting and tagging Centralia along Route 61,
just dirt mounds the county plowed
to block out the teenagers
with nowhere to go,
who sneak in like fireflies with cigarette butts
floating in the corpse of Atlas,
living dreams with groping hands,
collected, the way toys collect dead batteries.

Here we scribble *Welcome sinners! We have cookies*
on the night road full of heat fissures,
cracking spray paint, and lost lines:
I've gone to find myself; if I should get back before I return,
please ask me to wait
Centralia's roads lead nowhere now,
Just roads to vacancy and out of town.
With little honors, the last known survivors
remain, heavy and tired and marveling
at the emptiness on the outside, only shadows
of coal instead within their carbon-soaked lungs,
Tourists of graves, here we forget
how deep the mines run,
how long they will burn,
how ruined they remain
from the times the miners and Mennonites broke Earth,
when Alexander Rea engineered Locust Mountain Coal and Iron,

raised Centralia on a tomb of rock-men and trip-riders,
when the Molly Maguires shot him up
then they themselves swung down
by the gallows' mercy, out from the black
lung and canary's cage, into a holier promise
that the light at the end of the tunnel
was more than just another tunnel,
not just the ground hiding shame
shed and wept into the black soil
stained by what words we litter this world,

"This gallows is a family machine,
hanging day a holiday—

Centralia shows we're all coal crows,
Souls of black diamonds
waiting for the pickaxe
to chip us out and up
to the surface while the earth endures—
a seed and buried bodies,
where the teenagers graffiti Route 61
Here is the downside to the protest—
We may have to do some jail time,
As our children's children set fire to our past,
The trash burns, two hundred years
below teenagers praying
for something simple,
bored on tired truths, endlessness, and waiting,
they take a piss and linger
for the sun to rise.

Interstate 76 East

Colorado, I do not love as I should.
Instead, I search for a simpler state and ruin it with words.

You're too big; your sky is forever
too much for birds, your magnitude shades them invisible,
even to each other.

And in its vastness, I am the prey of sky,
and I will litter it with my debris, as if air
were a fear we need to fill— to name.

Adrienne and I drove for home, 4:30am breaking for Nebraska
before the sun accuses us of bailing east, without a penny or degree,
cowards under mountains, an empty apartment behind us.

The windshield kept me from the wind, from the air
that starts the sky in the Colorado dirt,
begging the Toyota and her radiator to hold over 1700 miles,

to my mother-in-law's guest room, the scroll of the road,
bare wood farm posts, open storm cellars, tractor fossil mementos
of settlers who never made gold but took homestead in the hills off Rt. 34.

In homes *almost* familiar and almost New Jersey,
almost shelter from a mother I can't call because she shipped me west
with no return address,

to Colorado, full of Hawthorn tree needles injecting.
She knows I'm no better & can bleed out like my father before me
who went down whimpering in the sun.

& I can't hide from the sun in this kind of sky, dead carried
in the shape of our face, graceless hunks of debt and doubt
that gave me my skin to fail in.

I remember in Boulder, Adrienne, you promised to teach me to ski,
but I couldn't even climb dry Poudre Canyon,
and failed to find ground, even for you, even for love,

Colorado, I cannot love you; I'm afraid of you,
& nothing simple can say how I am petrified
of both sky & the earth, both ready to devour.

Lewis Ginter Botanical Garden, Richmond, VA

My mother's knees soiled,
Calloused, down in the dirt,
sowing Forget-Me-Nots
and Black-eyed Susan's
in topsoil. Sweat in her hands,
cradling the seeds
like tiny bodies.
She plants them
in elegy of bloom,
but even among plants
we eat the young,
tear the seed from the leaf
to swallow before the fruition—
These are the lucky ones who go first,
either eaten or packed into the ground,
dark and soiled, seeing
if they choose the sun or solitude
in the yet-cold of March—
To branch skyward,
turn green, pregnant
and flowered, or to turn root,
immobile but for the buds.
she picks for pots,
displays the blossoms
in the living room
in floral exhibitions,
meant to make drywall
natural, perseverant,
a faux mockery of earth
dangled on plant hooks
hung still and unwatered,
we suffer—
until our own seedlings,
stripped from the branch
are devoured or buried—
In the end, food, either way.

Summer Vacation

At 19, I finally got around to sex, and I'm cool with the wait how a horse is cool with a full bladder. And on the day of the deed she ditches her parents and I shoplift a condom out of a porn store with a blue wrapper and unwrap her from her t-shirt as if breasts were a birthday present, her teeth with braces grate against the shaft of my penis, I gag at the taste of her vagina and we grind like we're assembling a bicycle but the instructions are in Mandarin as I try to penetrate with my eyes closed for mood lobbing lawn darts and planting a few pokes into her pelvis bruising our trust on the sacred tradition of teenagers misunderstanding each other's mechanics because sometimes when I kiss I mistake it for the act for chewing my spit dissolves her tongue looking for flavor mistaking her for my own biology mistaking color for flavor and flavor for color firm in my belief that if blow jobs were a color they would be rainbows and fireworks but I'm bad at being a man because I am bad at invasions I can't climax because she fails to be the women I was raised on women mistaken for porn store mannequins but she can't bend backwards or twist her tits back like a cat falling and photo'd mid-flop she doesn't slink her underwear doesn't match her bra, she gets her foot stuck in her sock winces from pain of the hymen snap and bleeds a trickle of blood that I am scared is made of death limping home on the one-good leg my father grinded from his body, as she lies still like a beautiful and boney pillow with too much truth in her biology and I'm making love to the rubber I mistake for her vagina, our sex set to "Me and Gun" because I am made a weapon by my want my want of my tongue tip to her nipple my finger tip to her clit as if I could tell the difference between a clit and a horse or a girl and joke whose punch-line is a real girl.

Vacation Slide #5

Incomplete. Heads cut from frame.
Vermont. "Maple Sweet" T-Shirts.
Who remembers this picture?
Was I even here at all?

Route 23, New Jersey

There will be no wakening./ When she wakens, she can't/ catch her own breath, so she yells/ for help. It comes in the form/ of sleep.
    ~Phillip Levine "For Country"

Of all the roads, this one leads home.
Working nights, driving in neutral
the impotence of the pedal
the motor distant, out of touch
it's just about momentum
dragging the body home to sleep
the half-sleep of sleeping
during the day where eyes never shut
tight or shut down continuing
to let in the sunlight
eyes dilate, blinking maybe
remembering your name
and place in space
body wants release
on the edge of the bed but waiting
for one last next thought
to permit rest but instead
while collecting the collateral
strains of muscles
& flat focus of the eyes
thoughts run on and go nowhere
like a bad sentence, broken syntax
the dead giving up on dying
for a long sentence of solitary
bodily confinement
where change is the only possibility
for rest because the routine
is what makes and breaks you
till the clock flashes the color of emergencies,
the phone rings like a drill

"your father is dead."

and last thought comes,
and nothing's left
but to go to sleep.

III.

Vacation Slide #6

We paused
snapped a quick shot
Behind, a child tearing
Lost, you're now safe in our picture
my dove

Liberty Science Center, Jersey City, New Jersey

For Ariadne

Science refuses to answer us why.
Why we love, why we have faith,
why blue soothes us or why we need
to make landscapes of sound and color,
even as we make symmetrical quarantined rooms.
Which may be why
by 4, I've taught my daughter to mourn,
mourn worn-out dresses, lost toys,
mourn the hundred scribbles and toddler-arts
expressing growth, maturing motor skills
climbing out of the *Touch Tunnel*,
dark-gripped, knowing nothing
but the tips of her fingers,
knowing the world both microscopic
and infinitely cosmic.
Because when I was there
I wanted to try everything,
But didn't dare
explore *Space Junk* or
climb *Skyscrapers*,
never brave enough for *Infection Connection*,
knowing loss like a layer of skin.
And even at 4, she worries when I will die,
when her home will be sold to strangers,
when funerals become flowers
blooming her memories in the fields behind her.
I am afraid I know science is the answer
and that answers murder the boundaries
of ourselves inch by inch into smaller universes,
and knowing is the death of possibility— hope
that physics may be broken, and every answer
may be right by its own honest means,
or that we were all present
in our very first cell, baby,
in our very first fingertip.

So maybe, when my age
she won't be writing poems at 2:18am
afraid of the breaking sensory deprivation,
afraid how clocks sound
when there is nothing else to listen to,
asking herself "why" to questions,
she was never allowed to ask.

The Poconos, Pennsylvania

We had that same argument about the car, the stuck clutch that grinds us
   forever in first gear.
We had the same argument about the apartment, crowded like cheap fish in a Walmart Aquarium,
   walls thin, we hear the neighbor fight with her dead mother.

We live in the Poconos, vacationland of the Living Dead, where they remember how Griffith and
   Lindbergh once dinned among us,
Where they remember the Union Houses, and the Lutheran Country Clubs, where they hunted and
   danced in Dionysian Wilds away from the city gray.
Before the march of Disney's Robots stamped out our sublime, and the weekenders came to take
   pictures of us dressed in rust.

We had that argument again, about living in a vacation, a spot billed on the quality of their iron lung,
Black lungs and sweep of miner's dust up from Carbon County, the taste of coal lingers on the
   tongue for generations,
Our grandfathers learned to limp young, always the crutch walking, who in tribute we eat
   cheap tea mix
just to taste something sweat casting Keystone cans to the side of the road along spent nicotine
   and motor oil.

All the while, we smile, with teeth, from the curb for the tourists—our iron lung—that we spatter
   with the spit of gratitude, slapped
as servers and gas station attendants, picking the fleas off route 80 coming to ski, raft, and dine
   off this dead dog town.

Adrienne, we had the same argument again, about when I dream and remember things

   that never happened—like you and I
flying in trash paper airplanes making for the sky, making for grander sights so near the sun, dining
   like cannibals on the natives

Las Vegas, Nevada

For Adrienne

when I am old, my love,
and the seasons are sick

with the threat of loss,
I will vacation in Vegas,

on the Strip, to pick showgirls.
She'll be death as promised,

in a pink boa,
she'll be a holy peacock

in this El Dorado-made
white lights and lipstick.

She'll dance to slots,
curl into my lap like a genie

I rub for wishes, deep throat
my ring finger and swallow.

She'll smell like candy and the womb.
breasts too small, teeth too white,

Curves too thin, all leg
and a birthmark. too wet—too perfect

too immortal to be a threat
like you, my love, so great a danger.

So let Vegas deliver me, baby,
too much a coward to love
and die last.

O'Hare International Airport, Chicago

The path,
routine
The flight,
mapped
The sky—
deep and without direction.

From a hard-plastic seat,
he reads the wall of clocks,
checks his watch,
& folds his newspaper into a rectangle.

Concourse polished, checked squares.
Symmetrical blocks of space.
Sky safely behind fields of glass.
Patterns in steel and tile.

From his hard-plastic seat,
he reads the wall of clocks,
checks his watch,
& folds his newspaper into a rectangle.

The call to flight—
a threat of open air
a threat of the fall,
the plummet and the earth
set to swallow with dark soil.

Palms wet,
he reads the wall of clocks,
checks his watch,
& folds his newspaper into a rectangle.

Beyond the terminals,
the world is broken
off a million curved lines
& unknowable destinations
But this space

inside
ends.
This space
is terminal.

Storyland, Glen, New Hampshire

Humpty Dumpty sits on a wall—
press his button to fall. Mother and Dad,
are you not glad we drove all this way?
It's Storyland day! It's Disney but small—
with chipped paint and all. This Cinderella is sad;
there's trash at the ball, with cheap meat and fries,
and a pink plushie prize and beanstalk ashtray.
Dad says this is gay, takes a dump in the stall
"Why come here at all?" He's dying and mad.
Screams we are bad, can't stand kids at play,
and wishes away these fairytale lies.
Mom does not cry, swallows the end of her wits.

And Grimm is this land, with no open skies.
We see our demise in these family time pits.

Legotown, New York

I dropped a Lego man in my grandfather's engine block,
An 81 Marquis, long and purple-brown gloss that he gives me
when I turn 19, once the stroke stole his legs and the left side of his face.
I'm 8 and fascinated with miniature places: inside couches, in the springs and beams of things,
in toy box dioramas of cotton swab palm trees, inside upside-down coolers
among islands of melted ice, and into the junk-drawers of the world.
When I was 8, I could have learned how to build, beyond Legos and plastic,
Learnt to build engines and cars, learned to repair pumps,
Learned to work cranes and machines made to work,
Labor with my hands, from a man whose toilets I flush when I turn 19
When the strokes stole his continence, stole his good-learned hands
that toiled 8 children, toiled free stuck mechanics,
knew the workings of physics with the touch of his hands,
knew how to engineer by the pulse of the machine, never learning to read,
whose toys weren't Legos but real steal and wood.
But I never learn, because even at 8,
I love being lost the way silence eats an echo,
I wanted to be in the inside; I wanted to see the world's assembly instruction
But I never learn, and stay a daydream, building with toy and words
& remain a miniature me, a child me who never learned what his hands taught,
what could fill a rusted world engines?
My tiny Lego man melts in the sump pan, breaks the oil pump with a toy
slag back to primordial plastic, in a forge of combustion and break-lines
of what I never learn—instead, I'm left wondering for how physics work
from books, having learned to read
too much—instead of searching
for his fingerprints
in the engine grease.

Vacation Slide #7

Grand Canyon—
Half a family—
mother and son
eyes panning
empty sky

What it was
I will not say
It is gone now

Anyway
the attraction here
has always been
what is missing

Disney's Hollywood Studios

My mother collects Mouse heads,
Displays them like trophies
in the forest of her work desk.
She taught her kids to play in the woods
with the Blue Fairy—
with the Cheshire Cat.

But at night, she dreams
Star Tours was made of cardboard.
She dreams of cracks in the sidewalks
and cartoons smoking in street clothes.
In her Great Movie ride,
Scarlet O'Hara, Ilsa Lund,
& Mary Poppins spoon feeds the sugar
to make the medicine go down.
The stars never look away,
and insomnia's a black space
where the magic is stuck, needs oil,
and is bolted through the foot.

Mickey is ever lost
in his imagination, Mom,
in his *Fantasmic,* a projected animation,
fire burned onto water,
so far removed that the tourists disappear
into their skinned-cartoon caps
Mickey doesn't seem to remember Toontown
was always a cartoon and that the suit was stuffed
with minimum wage workers fired
if they forget to smile.

And when Mom wakes up
the Wonderful World of Disney
loops on the T.V.,
the kids are no longer home
and the days keep marching

in an inescapable line
that leads everyone from the burning sun
and back to the parking lot.

Summer Vacation

I parked the car
on the grass, an old AV path,
tire tracks a memory sunk deep
in the mud of mid-August.
Summer almost over, I kill the headlights
and we sit and glow in the interior
cabin light. It's 2am and the old lake
lacks a name. Shy, it hides
its face in dew and fog,
hides itself from us,
seat belts still fastened,
staring into the dashboard.
I asked how her bulimia's going,
as if it were her favorite color,
she answered by rolling her sleeves down
to the rubber bands around her wrist,
tells me it was all my fault
and she's right—
it will be for decades to come.

This was the finality
we most likely deserved, alone
Her freckles are invisible at night.
She too hides her face in dew and fog
As she cracks open the car door,
climbs out and stares at the dog-day algae.
She'll be gone tomorrow
for Martha's Vineyard
family vacations I'm not invited to.
But I have my own vacations,
sets of dreams inside
the car out of radio stations,
static for all songs, I dream so deep
I forget my skin, watching her
through the windshield.
Past curfew, she kicks the clay
on the lakeside, the act so violent
nothing moves.

Teenagers love like a baby
learns to laugh, startled,
sounding out against joy.
In this dream, I follow her
from the car to the water's edge,
the surface of the lake
is made of outer space.
I strip to my underwear
And bare skinned dive,
water thick, green,
Scum-littered depth to surface,
I touch the whole pond,
touch the whole mountain,
the whole outer space,
become space ever-empty,
While she snaps the elastic
against the soft of her forearm.
See, love and loss
are the only training
for love and loss,
even if we're too naked
for night swimming.
So to keep from crying,
I drink the lake—
teenagers becoming
thistles and reeds rooted
to every body
of water either will ever
dare to bathe.

Six Flags, New Orleans

1.

This is the nature of echoes,
sound so much less than the call,
past reaching across space
no sound can cross.

2.

Flood a still lake. Rollercoaster bones
& concessions bob like litter in puddles.
Without signs. Without presence.
Vacant lot submerged in storm drain.

3.

Signs on restroom walls:
"Ladies and Gentleman"
"Aliens and Humans"
"Female Roaches to the left"
"Male Roaches to the right."
"Ghost" in the empty space.

4.

Clown face cracked and shattered,
threat of flesh under caked white.
Giant decapitated to the wet ground
still smiling a crippled grin.

5.

Broken glass upon ride controls.
Panel now sharp, Plexiglas fragments
cut at return attempts to ride.
Diamond dust blue.
Dead plastic switch.

6.

The swing chains—rain of rust—
still drift and spin in the wind.

Requiem squeaks.
Exit signs are dead metal
leading deeper and deeper into the high grass.

Seaside Heights, New Jersey

A blackout—
Ears ring over the silence
and I have gone where the lights go in the dark.
The vacuum chases this epitaph
for modern America in a power outage,
a still life after Sandy
pavement flooded with gentle streams.

          A green leaf glides in the current.

              The earth's deep breathing.

Ari's doll giggles from batteries
as she squeezes it to her chest,
from the carriage, as we walk
feeding her from an endless bottle.
She can't wait to feed the doll as I fed her,
there is so much love
we must fill our plastic with it,
Fill our blankets and pacifiers
with comfort, fill our toys
with our tender intent.
Even as pieces of the carnival float
In the wreckage of New Jersey
we love, even through plaster
love, even through clown noses
even through drowning arcades,
love the shape of twisted roller coasters
bent off the rail,
eaten by the loving ocean.
The doll laughs again,
just as my daughter
giggles in the bleak
carnival wreckage,
and it reminds me
how even materials and plastics
know the difference between
our lose and our love.

Interstate 95 North

The struggle itself towards the heights is enough to fill a man's heart. One must imagine Sisyphus happy.
          ~Albert Camus

This is the road to recover,
the way home, if there is one—
yellow-white halogens at night
bright enough to erase the world,
the swift and instant dance of snow.
It's 3: 15 am. We inch along, daring
the skittish wheel, bending with the
slips, skids, and controlled slides
of our tailgate caravan.
Radio off, no choice
but to listen
to the turning of our own motor,
the burn of the defogger,
the crunch of road salt.
There's no going back, no stopping,
only the dredging walk of traffic & plow trucks.
The past is what it is, insisting forward,
snow tunnels all into the present.
We pass dead cars, dug into unyielding drifts
by the strain of the march.
Stay awake. Keep moving.
Leave the dead where they lay.
We turn off at Marcus Hook,
abandon the caravan past Philly,
down roads trimmed in tree frost,
bone hands in a world dipped in nickel.
All paths lost & quick a falling sleet
the car pivots, back wheels outrun the front,
off the road, a crash soft as falling asleep,
leaves us crippled in the ditch.
Nothing left but to walk.
The snow falls thick,
ash of disintegrating sky,

faults of faithless clouds.
The cold is solid,
gunmetal ice wet against skin.
If we stop, cold seeps too deep,
the body furnace fails.
If we stop, the cold will burn,
nothing will ever feel warm.
It's 3:32 am. No change in the traction,
soles find black ice, frost tears both hands and knees
Still, we have to walk or become
the grey of everything.
& if we find home,
fingers shaking, numb,
jacket dripping snow
melted by the kerosene heat,
weathered hard as seashells,
we will find it walking,
find ourselves in the storm
both weather and frost bite,
both flesh and pain walking,
aching alongside the road,
alongside us, in the freeze
& the footsteps agony
yields to thaw.

The Animal Kingdom

My daughter walks beneath the *Tree of Life*,
roaring at lion carvings, flapping her arms
like a macaw. Stepping in fossils
she asks if Grandpa liked animals.
I tell her he could have if she likes,
for that's the joy of wild things,
that they are empty and flawed and beautiful.
She laughs and dances in a Mickey Safari hat.
The irony, Ariadne, was never the twine
we follow home but has always been
the make-believe we come to believe.
For even the lions know
they bleed to feed the trees,
& saturate the soil to bloom.
For even here, among the plastic
animals & plushies, there is real life,
even if we put plastic trees among lions
and expect the trees to bloom,
while the living ones are full
of empty branches. We mistake the litter
of leaves for ourselves, forgot how to feed
from the sun, forgot the liquid state of water,
& the current of clouds.
Yet it is the bare tips of branches
that we always return for,
so you, my love, can make yourself
a brave macaw and flutter
from our shaking limbs.

Gettysburg, Pennsylvania

no poems here—
only history,
sparse pine,
fields and clean air.
My daughter laughs
before she knows any words
dances with gravestones,
unaware of the corpses
buried beneath her feet,
inviting the dead
to join her none the less.

Epilogue

Cedar Point, Ohio

God is the tangential point between zero and infinity
　　　~Alfred Jarry

Climb the sky
into the sun
before we dive
metallic track
glide, scream,
pray,
gasping
exaltations—
songs.
curve
flip
twist,
confuse
the earth
for heaven,
heaven
for earth
until the car
comes to rest,
returned to the station
releasing the safety bars.

We collect our hats and glasses
　　　　step to the sidewalk,
　　　　　　　into a state of never embracing
　　　　　　　　　　screaming our more infinite falling
directionless,
eternal.

My Unending Thanks

There are so many beautiful souls that I would like to thank in regards to this book. Your voices of inspiration, encouragement, and support are carried not only in these words, but within the poet himself:

To the Poets whose guidance helped shape this book: Alicia Ostriker, Ross Gay, Patrick Rosal, Ellen Dore-Watson, Jane Mead, Michelle Greco, Shaun Fletcher, Darla Himeles, Richard Madigan, Bill Broun, Kim McKay, Jesse Burns, Roberto Carlos Garcia, Elliott batTzedek, Tara Yetter, Jude-Laure Denis, Mary Brancaccio, Yesenia Montilla, Cara Armstrong, Rick Carter, Freya Mercer, Sean Nevin, Jean Valetine, Sosha Pinson, Mathew Klitsch, Ysabel Y. Gonzalez, Daniel McLaughlin, Thomas Krivak, and Fadel K. Jabr.

And always the friends and family who took some or all of these trips alongside me: Amanda Bross, Eric Smith, Brandon Gilbert, Kevin Hayes, Paul Zahorosky, Amy Roberts, John McDonald, Jennifer Young, Elizabeth Barret-Walsh, Alison Breach, Diane Napoli, Mandy McShane-Gilbert, and Sue McShane.

Finally, and always, thank you Adrienne and Ariadne, with my heart. You are forever the way home.

Michael Lee Bross was born in July of 1977, a child of the disco and Star Wars era. He was raised in Wantage, New Jersey, in the shadow of High Point State Park and grew up a lover of fantasy, science fiction, music, mythology, and nearly all aspects of the written word. During his formative years, Michael was deeply affected by the death of his father, who was a victim of the HIV epidemic that struck during the tail end of the 20th century.

Before returning to school in his late twenties, Michael worked within a number of different careers: as a professional actor and stagehand, a bartender/waiter, a nurse's aide in developmental disability and brain trauma clinics, even a secretary for a children's sock company, but writing and poetry were an always present and guiding force in his life. Early on he found solace and inspirations in the works of Gary Snyder, Kurt Vonnegut, Ray Bradbury, Ursula LeGuin, Phillip Levine, Adrienne Rich, and Dean Young, to name just a few.

Michael's poetry is an examination of recklessness and spontaneity. He is fascinated by the catalytic power of language and its ability to push the boundaries of not only thought but experience as well. His approach is geared towards discovery, which at times leads him to the sincere, whilst other times to the odd and delightful. At the center of his work lies the driving force of questioning and introspection, leaving more interest in pursuit than the final destination.

He is also a graduate of the MFA in Poetry program at Drew University and is an active writer of both poetry and fiction. His first collection of poetry, the chapbook *Meditations on an Empty Stomach* was published in 2019 courtesy of Finishing Line Press. He is the recipient of the Martha E. Martin Awards for Poetry and Fiction, as well as the Jane Coil Cole Poetry Scholarship and the 2015 Arts by the People Chapbook Award. His work has been published in such periodicals as Lifeboat, Mobius Poetry Magazine, and Let's Talk Philadelphia.

Michael lives in Northeastern Pennsylvania, where he resides with his partner, Adrienne, and their daughter, Ariadne. He currently teaches composition and English at the University of Scranton.

www.ingramcontent.com/pod-product-compliance
Lightning Source LLC
Chambersburg PA
CBHW020336170426
43200CB00006B/409